nark Visitors

Shetland

Lindsey Porter

Published by
The Horizon Press

D.G. LESLIE
Lloyds TSB Scotland

Shetland Islands

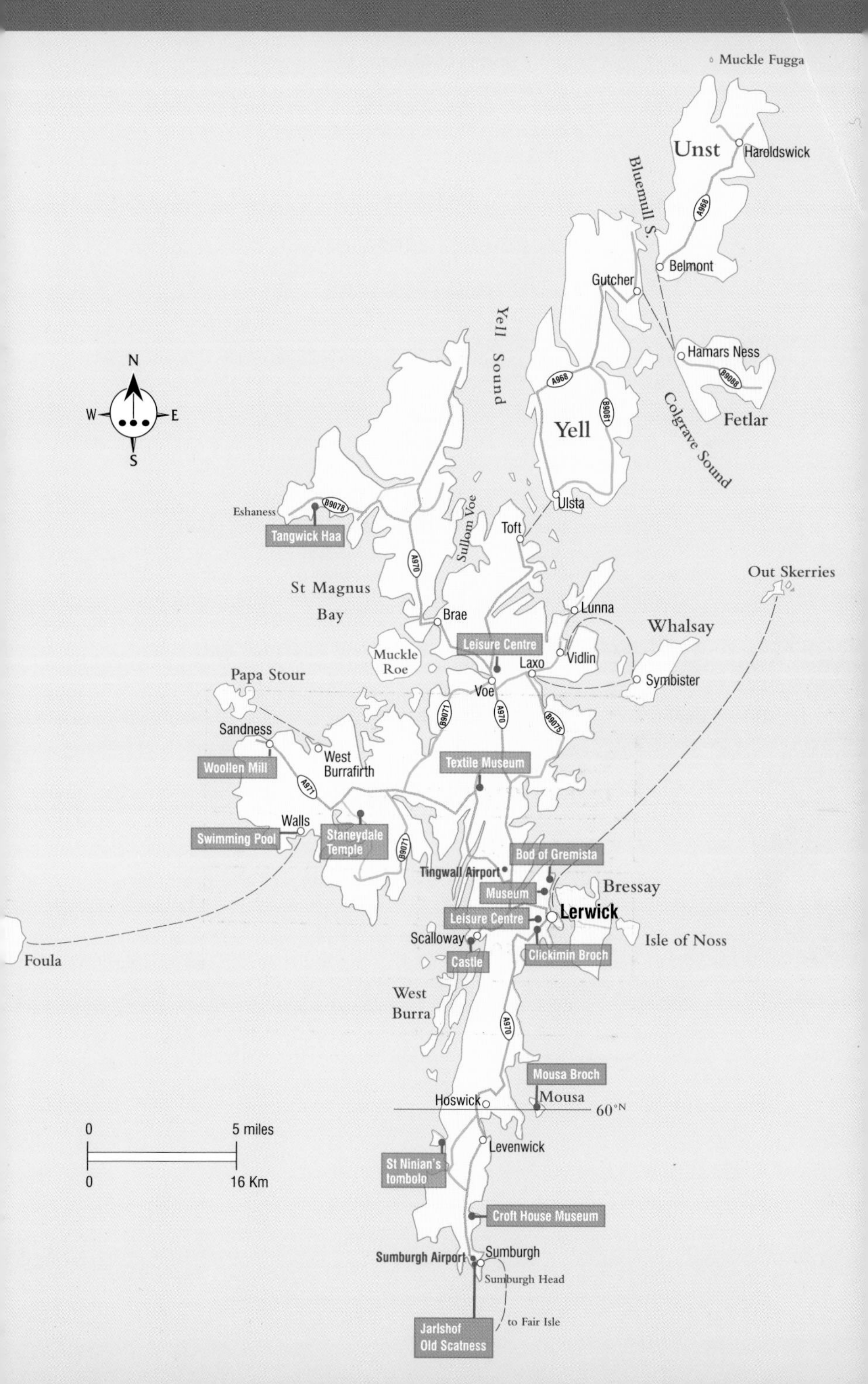

Published in the UK by:
Horizon Editions Ltd
Trading as The Horizon Press,
The Oaks, Moor Farm Road West, Ashbourne, Derbyshire DE6 1HD
e-mail books@thehorizonpress.co.uk

1st Edition

ISBN 978-1-84306-501-2

British Library Cataloguing in Publication Data:
A catalogue record for this book is available from the British Library

Printed by: Gomer Press Limited, Llandysul, Ceredigion, Wales

Cartography and Design: Mark Titterton

Picture Credits:

Page 2: Lerwick Harbour
Front cover: The Unst ferry at Gutcher
Back Cover top: St Ninian's tombolo; **bottom:** Heather west of Lerwick; **right:** Jarlshof

Kieran Murray: Aerial photography

All other photography by: Isobel Holbourne, Christine and Neil Mclean;
Helen Maurice Jones and Lindsey Porter

Contents

Top Tips

Jarlshof, Sumburgh – A continually occupied site from the Bronze Age to the 17th century

Old Scatness, Sumburgh – one of the UK's most important archeological sites

Mousa Broch, Mousa Island – Only complete Iron Age tower

Lerwick Museum – new and interesting range of galleries showing different periods of history

Boat Haven, Unst – good collection of historic boats

Kame of Foula, Foula Island – second highest cliffs in the UK

St Ninian's Island tombolo – especially when the sun is setting in the summer

Wildlife tour – lots of operators, either on the land or sea; well worth it, plus RSPB Reserves

Take an island ferry/flight – the island economies need it and all are of interest

Tangwick Haa Museum, West Mainland and the Old Haa, Burravoe, Yell – two good rural museums

Welcome to

The Shetland Islands

Sitting at the northern extremity of the nation, Shetland always seem to get a raw deal on the weather forecast. However, the islands receive the benefit of the Gulf Stream, which makes them five degrees or so better than one might expect for the latitude. Who would have thought that Shetland has more sunshine in summer than anywhere else in Britain? The rainfall is only 39in (99cm) and April to July the driest time to visit, June being the sunniest.

Opposite page: Clickimin Broch, near the Lerwick Leisure Centre and Tesco

Left: Latitude 60°N, Hoswick

Above: St Ninian's Isle tombolo

Below: Mousa Broch, the finest Iron Age broch surviving anywhere

In the same way that the UK Channel Islands owe some of their culture and language to their close neighbour France, so Shetland (and Orkney) can claim a similar experience with Norway. Its culture and custom, law and language owe an influence from invaders and settlers from north of Bergen (Rogoland province of Norway in particular). Owing allegiance to the King of Norway and later the King of Denmark is still evident particularly in place names and the dialect.

The original name of the Norse parliament – the Althing – lives on today in the placename Tingwall, where it was held. The actual site was probably on a promontory, previously an island in Tingwall Loch. It seems entirely appropriate that during the last war, when Norway was under German occupation, the 'Shetland Bus' still steamed in secret from Scalloway, Lunna etc to Norway. Today, Norwegian ships are a common sight at Lerwick, despite the closure of the ferry to Bergen in 2008.

The dialect is based on the Nord (sic) language with a liberal sprinkling of Scottish. Until the massive changes brought about by post-19th century technology, there were many indicators around, from buildings to boats, place names to practices which not only reflected a Nordic past but made and still makes both Shetland and Orkney something special. Compared to the Western Islands there isn't the same clan structure here or the Gaelic language either.

However, there is more to Shetland than just this. The Kame of Foula, out to the west, has the highest cliffs in the UK, second only to St. Kilda. The bird population is something to crow about too. Oil-based industry and transportation (plus gas) has invigorated North Sea hugging ports and piers, bringing a boost to flagging economies and employment opportunities. It has certainly stemmed island depopulation in several instances.

That iconic symbol of prehistoric Scottish settlements, the broch, has its finest surviving example in Shetland, at Mousa Island. Here, according to the *Orkneyinga Saga*, a couple from Norway spent a prolonged honeymoon in 1153. It is largely complete to this day. In fact the lady was taken against her will, or at least that of her son. He followed the couple to Mousa and realised that a siege would probably be fruitless. Wisdom prevailed and the issues were sorted out! Peter Guy in his book *Walking the Coastline of Shetland, No 6 South Mainland* records that in c. 900AD a couple eloping to Iceland from Norway were shipwrecked and took refuge at Mousa broch, even getting married there. There are some 500 or so in Scotland (none elsewhere) and Shetland can account for 141 brochs or possible brochs. It also has

Mousa Broch

Lerwick

The Shetland capital is Lerwick. It is the only major town, with a population of c. 7,500. It is about one-third of the total island population of 22,000 and half as many again live within ten miles of it.

Despite its small size, it enjoys all the facilities and atmosphere of mainland communities much larger in size. Its waterfront bustles with activity, it harbour sheltered by Bressay Island just offshore. In the town centre are the offices of Visit Shetland where you can sort out queries, bookings etc.

Similar to many of the smaller islands, Lerwick enjoys a superb leisure centre at Clickimin. It also has a theatre, art gallery and a good range of shops and restaurants. The ferry from Aberdeen on Scotland's mainland docks here and the airport is just 23 miles (39km) away.

Lerwick is not a large town, which means that it is easy to explore and find the shops and facilities you may need. The main street is Commercial Street, now largely traffic free. The banks are here, but few main UK High Street outlets.

Hay's Dock, a short distance beyond what remains of the castle, is definitely worth a stroll away from the town centre. The museum and art gallery is a worthy place to visit and there are a few vintage boats in the small harbour adjacent. The café doubles as a restaurant in the evening, giving a modern environment overlooking Bressay Sound to fine dining.

The museum highlights many finds from around the various islands. There are exhibits from Stone Age times and even a recreated couple of rooms of a house of c. 1760. This is an absorbing collection, well worth going to see. Allow plenty of time to see what there is – you will need all of it!

Continuing out of town past the Bus Station (and the turn right to Hay's Dock) just past the Scottish Power Electricity generating plant is a further right turn to the Bod of Gremista. This former house was where Arthur Anderson, who founded the P & O Shipping Company, was born in 1792. The property was used for storage and was restored a few years ago, with a significant donation from P & O, whose flag flies from the flag pole. The building was erected in 1780 and was used for fish curing and storage on the ground floor, with accommodation above for the manager.

On the road to the airport is the large, circular Clickimin Broch. Reduced in height, it none-the-less is worth a visit to see what home looked like 2,000 years ago to Lerwick's then community. Across the adjacent small lake is the red-roofed, well appointed Leisure Centre: late afternoon is probably the best time to visit the broch if you are looking for good photographs as the sun sets.

The boats to Bressay and Out Skerries leave from adjacent to the Port Authority Building, adjacent to the Albert Dock. Many narrow passages thread their way down to the waterfront but the commercial quay is now out of town.

Lerwick has a disc parking system for the shopping area. These are obtainable from the Tourist Information Centre or most shops. There is free car parking available in Market Street, Upper Hillhead and Church Road.

Bressay Ferry, Lerwick

Above left: Lerwick Museum *Above right: Lerwick Castle*

The RNLI shop and harbour beyond

Preserved craft at Hay's Dock Lerwick Museum

North-East, Northmavine and the West

Four miles (6km) north of the airport (Tingwall), the B9075 bears left off the A970, the island main north-south spine road. The B-road provides a circuit around South and North Nesting. It is scenic, with a few villages en-route and good views, especially around Gletness at the end of the promontory east of Cat Firth.

The B9075 reaches the B9071 at Laxo, where the ferry leaves for Whalsay Island, except when strong south easterly winds force it to switch to the much more sheltered port at Vidlin, where the ferry for the Out Skerries is based. Beyond Vidlin is the village of Lunna at the neck of a peninsula bearing the same name. Lunna was the base (until 1943) for the secret 'Shetland Bus', ferrying men and supplies into German-held Norway and bringing out men on the run from the Gestapo. It was run from Lunna House. The peninsula runs up to Lunna Ness, a SSSI because of its otter population. This is wild country, a haven for wildlife but you are clearly going to see more of the birdlife than the illusive otters!

Between Vidlin and Laxo is The Cabin Museum, a large eclectic collection of war memorabilia and collectables. What started as a small hobby grew into a huge collection now housed in a purpose built museum. Nearby, Lunna Kirk is Shetland's oldest church still in regular use. It dates from 1753 but incorporates a much older structure.

From Lunna Ness it is 8 miles (13km) as the crow flies to Sullom Voe oil terminal. A different world one could hardly imagine so close to such serenity and unspoilt landscape. Sullom Voe is now the 10th largest UK port in terms of annual tonnage, handling 3.3% of all UK traffic. It is also the 2nd largest crude oil port in the UK handling 13.6% of traffic – nearly 20 million tonnes of it. From the North Sea and the Atlantic, oil reaches here by pipeline and Sullom Voe provides the sea lane by which it is exported.

By comparison, Shetland's 50-million pound deepwater fishing industry for mackerel, haddock, herring and blue whiting amounts to c. 60,000 tonnes per annum, with mackerel accounting for over 51,000 tonnes. (Figures from *Shetland in Statistics*) Yet both contribute much to the island economy and help to sustain the 'fragile' communities on some of Shetland's islands.

The north-west corner of the Mainland is the parish of Northmavine, which is almost separated from the Mainland at Mavis Grind. Here the Atlantic has almost cut through to the southern tip of Sullom Voe.

Northmavine is a large area, with much of it unspoilt wilderness with a dramatic coastline of cliffs, caves and stacks.

The highest point is Ronas Hill, which rises to 1,476ft (450m). The views, on a good day, are stunning fully reaching the southern tip of the Shetland Mainland, out to Foula in the west, to the tip of Unst and the Out Skerries too. There are coastal walks and also the B9078 which extends out to the Esha Ness Lighthouse at the parish's western tip, taking in the communities of Hillswick and Braewick on the way. At the northern end of Northmavine is an area of lochans and good freshwater fishing.

Much of the area consists of moorland and rough grazing. It is largely not too scenic – even a little monotonous, broken in August by the purple flowers of the heather.

Other than the impressive stretches of coastline and the spectacular islet known as The Drongs, near to Hillswick, the chief place to visit, from the point of view of an attraction, has to be Tangwick Haa Museum at Eshaness. This house was built in the late 17th century, by the Cheyne family who owned an estate here.

By the 1960s it was roofless. Still in the same family, it was given to the Shetland Islands Council who restored it. In addition to local memorabilia, it has an impressive room layout on the first floor. Sir Walter Scott stayed here and it gives a good idea of what the house was like. There is also a silk wedding dress, dating from the 1840s, on show, which was used at that time at a Cheyne family wedding.

West Mainland, also referred to as Westside, consists of the peninsula south of St. Magnus Bay. It is pierced by several fjord-type sounds or voes, and dotted by many lochans (small lakes) in a mixed landscape of croft and moorland. Despite the presence of several communities, it has managed to maintain an air of solitude, often endowed with sunshine, especially in summer and when south-easterly winds are blowing.

It shares a common heritage with other parts of mainland Shetland and nearby islands and a coastline of dramatic cliffs, sheltered voes and low-lying hills harbouring evidence of a 5,000-year occupation.

Exploration on foot or by car is worthwhile and your choice will no doubt be dictated by the time available. The information centre at Walls (Waas) can provide help for walkers. It is to be found at The Baker's Rest, which is above the bakery, next door to the shop and post office. Produce from the bakery can be purchased in the tearoom, including Shetland 'Oaties', a traditional hard biscuit made from oats. The spine road from Bixter in the east to Sandness (on the coast and south of Papa Stour Island) plus the branch to Walls, has numerous lanes leading to the coast.

However, not all offer a circular route to follow.

Just beyond Bixter at Park Hall (the house is now a ruin but retains its elegant front façade) take the road to Sand (left) if you wish to explore a more circuitous route. Take a detour (again to the left) to Sand and where there is a sign for Innersand, go right to reach the shore and a car park. Behind a disused house is a churchyard with only the chancel arch remaining of what would have been the east window of a 12th century church, falling into disrepair in the 1760s.

Returning to the road you turned off, go left and continue on through Reawick with its reddish-granite sandy beach. Follow signs to Walls, reaching the main road at Bridge of Walls. This circuitous route offers a glimpse of rural solitude characteristic of much of West Mainland. However, for the walker or bird watcher, it must be a haven.

At Sandress is Jamieson's woollen mill. Here they dye, spin and knit 100% Shetland wool. It is in fact, the only place that can claim this accolade. They also have a shop on site and will explain the production process. Jamieson's have an outlet at 93/95 Commercial St, Lerwick. ☎ 01595 693114

Aith on the north-west coastline of West Mainland has the area's Community Leisure Centre and there is a swimming pool at Walls. Aith also has the most northerly RNLI lifeboat station, one of two in Shetland (with Lerwick). There are shops at Aith, Bixter and Walls and also fuel in these three villages.

Above: Voe Harbour

Below: Toft, for ferries to Yell

Opposite page: Tangwick Haa Museum interior

Central Mainland

This area consists of part of the main southern peninsula which stretches from the Weisdale area in the north to Scalloway in the south. To the east is Lerwick, with Scalloway, older by far, on the west coast. The latter was the main community before the ascendancy of the equally sheltered Lerwick which was better positioned for European trade. However, the older administrative area of the Norse settlers was at Lawting Holm at the head of Tingwall Loch. The parliament, known as the Althing, met here.

From Lerwick, take either of the two roads towards Scalloway. To explore the area, go north on the B9074 towards Tingwall. The Central Mainland area is noted for its stunning scenery and memorable views, trout lochs and rich flower-filled meadows in the summer. The route follows the road to Tingwall, Whiteness and Weisdale before joining the A971 to return south back to Tingwall.

On the west side of the Mainland, the voes are long and narrow and this is continued by the islands of West and East Burra and also Trondra, the nearest to Scalloway. Fault lines weakened the geology here and the sea has taken advantage of it. The remaining surface lands being of more resistant rocks have stubbornly blunted the erosive power of Atlantic storms and glaciation. These faults run a little east of north and track up towards the north of Shetland, influencing the west shoreline of Sullom Voe, for instance.

The islands are connected with bridges from the Mainland, with little villages, lovely beaches and yet more memorable scenery and views out to Foula, 25 miles (40km) out to the west. In the churchyard of the ruined St. Laurence Church at Papil, on the south end of West Burra, are three early Christian carved stones – or were, two now being replicas. The originals are in the Shetland Museum at Lerwick.

Scalloway is Shetland's second town, supporting a population of around 2,000 people. It is a busy fishing port with a long and interesting heritage. Its castle of 1599, is a tall and gaunt reminder of more troubled times. It is a high building, now roofless. None-the-less, a key is available from the Scalloway Hotel about half a mile or so along the sea front. Access is free. Scalloway is only 15 minutes away by car or 20 minutes on the bus from Lerwick.

Troubled times did not end centuries ago as the 'Shetland Bus' memorial reminds us. Erected to commemorate those lost on raids from here to Norway in WWII, it is shaped like a small version of

Mousa Broch. The nearby Norway House was the town's base for the secret raids, taking men and supplies to help the Resistance. Scalloway's Museum has a display on the 'Shetland Bus'.

The Shetland Bus

During WWII, boats ferried arms, ammunition, other supplies and men into Norway, bringing out refugees and others fleeing the Gestapo. Using armed camouflaged fishing boats, ten were destroyed by 1943 and the operation was in danger of being wound up. A total of 44 men were killed, all except five aged below 30 years of age.

The US Navy stepped in and gave the Norwegian Navy Independent Unit three submarine chasers. Between October 1943 and May 1945, a further 150 missions were undertaken without loss. One of these three vessels, the *Hitra*, survives at the Navy Museum, Horten, Norway. After initially being based at Lunna, operations were carried out from 1943 in Scalloway, under the up-most secrecy.

The Shetland Bus Memorial, Scalloway

Above: Scalloway Castle

Above left: 12th century church remains, near Innersand Above right: Reawick beach

Above: Dyeing at Jamieson's Woollen Mill, Sandness

Above: Aith Harbour

South Mainland

South of Central Mainland is a long, narrow peninsula running up to 30 miles (48km) down to Sumburgh Head (the actual length varies from where you take the top to be!). Few places are more than a mile or so from the sea. There are many attractive, sandy beaches and a rich heritage of occupation and land use. As elsewhere, seabirds and seals abound; the otter is there too, but more illusive. Land-based birds and Shetland ponies add to the variety of local wildlife.

The Croft House Museum, a restored homestead with a watermill nearby gives a good impression of the way of life a hundred or so years ago. The larger and more powerful Quendale watermill shows how production techniques moved on from earlier, more subsistence-based ways of working. It is the only surviving overshot waterwheel-powered mill in Shetland, built in 1867.

South Mainland has some of the nation's finest Iron Age remains. Uniquely, Mousa Broch is virtually complete, whilst violent storms removed the sand cover hiding the remarkable villages at Old Scatness and Jarlshof (a modern name apparently invented by Sir Walter Scott). Both sites are within a mile of each other and a visitor centre preserves artefacts from the sites next to the Sumburgh Hotel. Jarlshof has remains dating from the Bronze Age up to the 17th century and includes an entire Viking village. Because of the continuity of useage, Jarlshof is one of the most important sites in the UK. At Old Scatness, you have a conducted tour, with much detail explained which you would otherwise miss.

Another important archaeological find occurred in 1958 on St. Ninian's Isle at a dig in a Celtic chapel. A schoolboy found a hoard of silver bowls and ornaments, carefully crafted in about 800AD. These now reside in Edinburgh, with only replicas on display in the Shetland Museum at Lerwick. Is it time the originals came back to Shetland now that the islands have a fine home in which to accommodate them?

Old Scatness and Jarlshof give a good impression of Iron Age communities and their way of life. So much so, that they are the top visited sites of any fee-charging attractions in Shetland. Equally important, but located on Mousa Island, off the east coast, is Mousa Broch. Only found in Scotland and one of c. 500 (of which 141 brochs, or potential brochs, survive in Shetland). A short boat trip from Leebitton at Sandwick soon delivers you to Mousa Island. There is also a late evening trip to witness the storm petrels after dusk returning to nest by the hundred in the walls of the broch.

The boat returns at 12.30 am from the island.

Mousa Broch is 43ft (13m) tall and 50ft (15m) in diameter at its base. There are galleries and a staircase within the thickness of the wall to the top.

The RSPB has two nature reserves in the southern end of the peninsula. At Sumburgh Head, beyond the airport, the reserve protects large colonies of seabirds, easily observed from the lighthouse. If you look over the nearby wall above the cliffs you can see nesting seabirds including puffins closeby. However bear in mind that the puffins leave the islands in late August. The other reserve is at Spiggie Loch, a wildfowl refuge near Scousburgh, about 5 miles (8km) to the north-west of Sumburgh Head. See also Mousa Island below.

Spiggie Loch is signposted to the left as you drive north. There is a good sandy beach there consisting of fine sand. The lane past Spiggie Beach continues on to St. Ninians Island, only a short distance further up the road. It is connected to the mainland by a spit or bar (known locally as an ayre). However, where they join two separate pieces of land, they are called a tombolo. The one here is large and composed of fine sand.

In addition to creating two lovely beaches back to back, so to speak, its two curved beaches create a distinctive and unusual form to the tombolo itself. Looking at it from St. Ninian's Isle with the sun on your back forms a lasting and impressive memory.

Immediately to the south of Spiggie Beach is Spiggie Loch, now a RSPB nature reserve popular with migrating whooper swans and greylag geese heading south from the Arctic. In the summer, the warm climate on this west coast is favoured by other birds including great skuas and arctic terns.

On the way back to Lerwick, the Sandwick area hosts the Hoswick Visitor Centre and tourist information point. It has a café and a large display on weaving and lace making. It also has a large wireless collection. Adjacent is the factory of Laurence J Smith, weavers and lace makers, who have a shop selling their products. The Queen visited the works in 1969. Adjacent to the Mousa Island ferry are the Sandayre boat sheds, now restored and housing various displays and a four-oar flit boat now preserved and presented by Tom and Cynthia Jamieson, proprietors of the Mousa ferry. Sandwick is also the site of the area's swimming pool.

On Mousa Island is a further RSPB reserve. The island has a colony of some 6,000 storm petrels, several other species of sea birds and some 400 common seals.

Jarlshof, occupied for 6,000 years

Above left: Recreated roundhouse, Old Scatness   Above right: Jarlshof

W = wet weather attraction

Places to Visit

Lerwick

Bod of Gremista *W*
Gremista (north of Lerwick ferry terminal, Holmsgarth)
☎ 01595 694386; or Shetland Museum 695057
18th century restored house
Open: Jun-mid Sept, 10am-1pm & 2-5pm. Free admission

Clickimin Broch
Southern end of Clickimin Loch, south of Lerwick. Substantial remains, reduced in height, possibly 2,000 or more years ago. Easy access off the Sumburgh airport road, heading south, just beyond Tesco on the right hand side. Free admission

Shetland Times
Has shop selling books on Shetland/walking guides etc

Clickimin Leisure Centre *W*
Lochside
☎ 01595 741000
Large attraction including water-based complex and sports hall

Isleburgh Exhibition of Shetland Crafts & Culture *W*
Isleburgh Community Centre, King Harald St
☎ 01595 692114
Open: mid-summer, Mon, Wed, Thurs 7-9.30pm
Demonstrations of knitwear, spinning and other crafts (incl. Fair Isle and openwork lace knitting)

Shetland Museum & Archives *W*
Hay's Dock, ZE1 0WP
☎ 01595 695057
5* attraction plus café/restaurant
☎ 01595 741569
www.shetlandmuseumandarchives.org.uk

Open: daily, Mon-Fri 10am-5.30pm; Sat 10am-5pm; Sun noon-5pm. Free
High quality restaurant open in the evenings and lunchtime. Absorbing array of galleries of displays of various periods of history; art gallery

Up Helly Aa Exhibition ***W***
St. Sunniva Street
Open: mid-May to mid-Sep; Tues & Sat 2-4pm; Tues & Fri 7-9pm

Garrison Theatre/Cinema ***W***
Market Street
☎ 01595 743843

North East Shetland

Lunna Kirk
The oldest church still in use in Shetland, at Lunna

Lunna Ness
A site of special scientific interest (SSSI) to protect its otters

Lunna House
HQ of the Shetland Bus operation until 1943. Now a B&B

The Cabin Museum ***W***
Vidlin
☎ 01595 694891/ 01806 577232
Open: Tues, Thurs, Sat, Sun 1pm-5pm

Other Information

Swimming Pool ***W***
Brae
☎ 01806 522321

Voxter Outdoor Centre
☎ 01806 522464

Ferry to Out Skerries
Vidlin to Symbister (Whalsay)
☎ 01806 566259 and Out Skerries
☎ 01806 515226

Petrol: Brae, S. Nesting, Vidlin & Voe
Shopping: Brae, Firth, S. Nesting, Vidlin & Voe.

Northmavine

Tangwick Haa Museum ***W***
Eshaness, ZE2 9RS
☎ 01806 503347
Open: 1st May-Sep, 11am-5pm
Includes Tourist Information Point
Free admission
Large walled garden and picnic area

Other Information

Petrol: Ollaberry
Shopping: Hillswick & Ollaberry

West Mainland

Staneydale Temple
Largest Stone Age remains in Shetlands
Situated above east end of Scutta Voe, east of Walls (Waas)

The Baker's Rest Tearoom
Walls Bakery, Walls ZE2 9PF
☎ 01595 809308
Open: May-Oct, Mon-Sat, 10.30am-4pm
Tea Room plus sales of Shetland 'Oatie' and other Shetland biscuits etc

Jamieson's Woollen Mill
Sandness ZE2 9PL
☎ 01595 870285
Visitors welcome
Open: mill & shop 9am-1pm & 2-5pm
Mail order: ☎ 01595 693114

Other Information

Tourist Information Point
The Baker's Rest, Walls (Waas)
☎ 01595 809308

Petrol/Shopping: Aith, Bixter & Walls (Waas)

Swimming Pool: Walls (Waas)
Ferry to Papa Stour: West Burrafirth
☎ 01595 810460

Ferry to Foula: Walls (Waas)
☎ 01595 753254

Central Mainland

Bonhoga Gallery ***W***
Weesdale ZE2 9LW
☎ 01595 745750
Includes a café
Open: Tues-Sat, 10.30am-4.30pm; Sun noon-4.30pm

Scalloway Castle (H.S.) ***W***
☎ 01856 841815
Free Admission

Scalloway Museum
Open: May-Sep, Mon-Sat, times vary and closed at midday
Free Admission

Shetland Jewellery
Soundside, Weisdale ZE2 9LQ
☎ 01595 830275

Other Information

Petrol: Burra, Weisdale
Shopping: Hamnavoe, Scalloway, Whiteness, Weisdale

South Mainland

Croft House Museum ***W***
Nr Boddam
☎ 01950 460557
Open: May-Sep, 10am-1pm & 2-5pm

Hoswick Visitor Centre ***W***
Hoswick, nr Sandwick
☎ 01950 431406
Open: 1st May-30th Sept; weekdays 10am-5pm; Sun 11am-5pm

Jarlshof
Sumburgh Head
☎ 01950 460112
Open: Mar-Oct, daily 9am-5.30pm

Mousa Broch
☎ 01950 431367
Boat from Leebitton (see below), Apr-Sep
info@mousaboattrips.co.uk

Old Scatness Broch & Iron Age Village
North of Sumburgh Airport
☎ 01595 694688/ 01950 461869
Open: May-Oct, Sun-Thurs 10am-5pm
In winter by arrangement
In recent years this has been one of the largest archaeological excavations in Europe. Great for children.

Quendale Watermill Dunrossness ***W***
☎ 01950 460969 (when mill open)
Open: Apr-Oct, daily 10am-5pm
Visitor Centre, craft shop & café. Video of original mill in use; displays of crafting tools and artefacts. Situated off A970 just north of Sumburgh airport

RSPB Reserves
Contact: RSPB, East House, Sumburgh Head Lighthouse
Virkie, Shetland ZE3 9JN
☎ 01950 460800

Mousa Island

RSPB Mousa Nature Reserve
c/o RSPB, East House, Sumburgh Head Lighthouse, Virkie ZE3 9JN
☎ 01950 460800
Open: mid-Apr to mid-Sep
6,000 pairs of storm petrels breed here, not overlooking 400 common seals and many other seabirds.

Mousa Boat Trips
Leebitton, Sandwick
☎ 01950 431367/07901 872339
April to mid-Sept
Day or night time trips to see the storm petrels returning to their nest sites; subject to weather/sea permitting.
10% discount for RSPB members. Look out for seals, porpoises and whales on your trip.

W = wet weather attraction

Above: Quendale Watermill

Above left: Heather in bloom in August and former peat-cutting site, A970 west of Lerwick Above right: Shetland ponies, Levenwick

Above: The Boat Museum, Sandayre, with a preserved 4-oar flit boat. It is adjacent to the ferry quay for Mousa Island.

Above: Spiggie Loch (left), an RSPB nature reserve

Bressay & Noss

Bressay

Situated ten minutes away from Lerwick is the island of Bressay, sheltering Shetland's capital from the sea. If time is restricted, this is the most convenient island to visit from the Shetland Mainland and you are immediately aware of a quieter and slower pace of life. Check that the timetable suits your requirements.

Bressay is 7 miles (11km) by 3 miles (5km). Taking your car enables you to explore more quickly and easily but if time allows then there is some good walking to be enjoyed along the coast and also on a circular coastal walk around the small adjacent isle of Noss. However, you are requested not to drive on un-metalled roads and keep your dog/dogs on a lead. In fact the concessionary paths exclude all dogs, whether on a lead or not.

Most of the island is made of Old Red Sandstone, which has resulted in the cliffs that house thousands of sea birds. This stone also provided the building stone and roof flagstones for Lerwick.

Bressay has a population of c. 350 and many commute to work in Lerwick, hence a frequent and largely convenient ferry timetable. The ferry docks at Maryfield where the Bressay Heritage Centre is situated. It also houses the Tourist Information Centre. Much of the community is to be found on the more sheltered west side of the island. The interior is chiefly moorland, rising to a height of 742ft (226m).

Looking across at the pier is the early Georgian, Palladian fronted Gardie House, built in 1724 and now the home of Shetland's Lord Lieutenant. The road south along the coast takes you to Mail (from the Norse word for sand). Here you can find a shop, post office, church and petrol station. The road continues on to Kirkabister, now without its kirk (church). It goes on to the island's prominent landmark, the Bressay lighthouse built in 1858. Some of the buildings here are now self-catering holiday lets. ☎ 01595 694688; e: info@shetland amenity.org

The road east from Mail leads to the ferry for Noss and also goes to Setter, where a track continues to the deserted village of Cullingsbrough.

Here at the ruins of the 10th century St. Mary's Chapel is a replica of the famous Bressay Stone found in 1864 with impressive Pictish carving. The original is in the Shetland Museum, Lerwick. There are WWI 6-inch guns extant on the headlands on the far north-east and south-east.

A recent attraction is the relocation of the burnt mound from Cruester to the Bressay Heritage Centre. It was in danger of being destroyed by the sea and in 2008, each stone was carefully numbered following excavation. There seems to be a great many of them, but they have all been carefully recreated on the new site. What precisely a burnt mount was is still not clear. What is known is that fires seem to have been used to heat water. The adjacent heritage centre has an exhibition of local matters and a nice recreation of a "ben-room", a domestic room of the 1960s. The public toilets are adjacent to the Centre.

Noss Island

Bressay has a close neighbour on its east coast – the Isle of Noss. It is now a National Nature Reserve and has a seabird breeding colony of some 150,000 birds and chicks, including 45,000 guillemots and 8,500 gannets. See below for access details.

The island is privately owned by the Garth Estate and run as a sheep farm. However, there is a 5-mile, 8km coastal path, giving access to stunning scenery, a wide number of bird species and abundant flowers. The island has a visitor centre. Look out for seals, porpoises and even whales.

If the weather does not permit the sailing of the boat to pick you up, a red flag is flown. The island is one of the most popular paid attractions in the Shetlands. Dogs are not allowed on Noss, however. You park at the end of the road at an obvious car parking area looking down onto Noss. You have to make your way down to the quay. Ring ahead if disabled. Take adequate footwear and warm clothes as the weather may change after arrival.

Getting There

Regular ferries from Lerwick, crossing takes 10 minutes. You are not able to book this service in advance. ☎ 01595 743974 (voice bank)
Every hour from 11.15am to 11pm (later on Fri & Sat nights)
Noss Ferry, ☎ 0800 1077818, late May-Aug. Island open: 10am-5pm (not Mon or Thurs). Visitors should wait by sign on Noss Sound and the boat will come to pick you up.

Accommodation

Booking Agency – Visit Shetland
☎ 08701 999440

Places to Visit

Bressay Heritage Centre *W*
Maryfield
☎ 01595 820750 (answering machine for opening times) or
☎ 01595 693434
Open: Tues, Wed, Fri, Sat 10am-4pm; Sun 11am-5.30pm.
Free admission

Cruise from Lerwick
(adj. Port Authority Building)
Details available from Lerwick Tourist Information Centre
☎ 01595 693434
April-Sep, weather permitting

Concessionary coastal path in south and southwest of island

Northern Lights Holistic Spa
☎ 01595 820257
www.shetlandspa.com
Ensuite accommodation or day visits

Above: Gardie House, Maryport, Bressay

Below: Bressay Visitor Centre and re-erected burnt mound in foreground

Noss ferry heading for Bressay

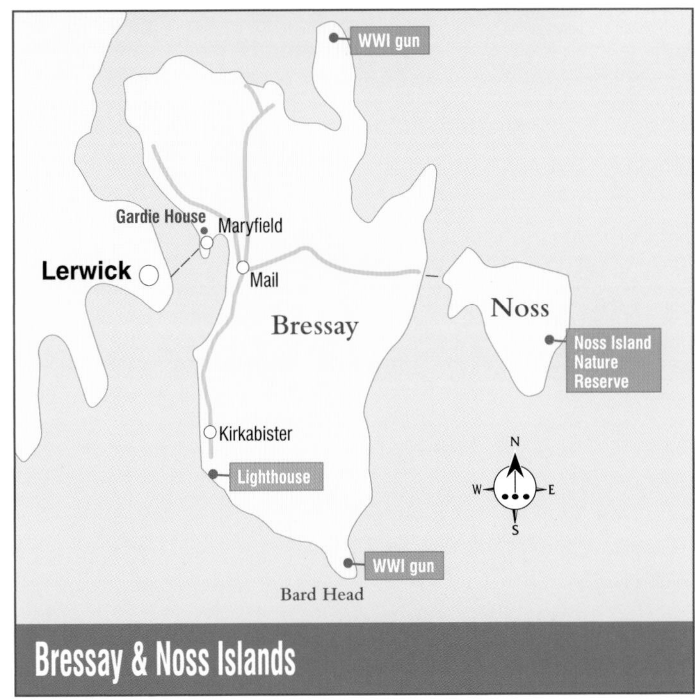

Fetlar

This is Shetlands fourth largest island after Mainland, Yell and Unst.

It has always been known for its fertility and had a high population prior to the clearances.The population is now under a hundred. The fertility has given the island's wild flowers splendour not matched anywhere else in Shetland.They are at their best from April to August and there are c. 300 different species.

You can learn more about the wildlife, history and archaeology of the island at the Fetlar Interpretive Centre at Houbie. It also has displays on two of the island's principal houses, Brough Lodge, built in c. 1820 and Leagarth House built in 1900 and the home of Sir William Watson Cheyne, a prominent surgeon who worked with Lister on pioneering antiseptic surgery.

Near Aith is Grant's Grave, excavated by the Time Team. It turned out to be a Viking boat burial, although the boat had rotted away. Nonetheless its outline was still visible. Much older is the Finnigert Dyke, a large stone wall of Bronze Age provenance. It runs from north to south and divided the island into two.

Oral tradition has it that Gruting was where the Vikings first landed in Shetland.

Fetlar has impressive cliffs near Gruting on the north-east coast and sandy beaches in the same area and also near Brough Lodge on the west coast and at Funzie (pronounced Finnie) on the east coast.

There are six sites of Special Scientific Interest (SSSIs) on Fetlar.

Getting There

There is no public transport or petrol/diesel available for vehicles on Fetlar.

Ferry from Gutcher, on Yell (25 minutes) to Hamars Ness on Fetlar and from Belmont (Unst) to Hamars Ness. Bookings ☎ 01957 722259

Voicebank ☎ 01595 743971

Ferry office open: Mon-Sat 8.30am-4.45pm, closed Sunday.

Note: bookings not accepted where the travelling time through Yell (between Ulsta and Gutcher terminals) is less than 25 minutes.

A bus leaves Viking bus station, Lerwick at 8am daily, except Sunday. At Ulsta on Yell, a bus service goes to Gutcher for the ferry to Belmont on Unst. In addition there is an additional bus leaving Lerwick at 4pm on Tuesdays and Thursdays with connecting ferries for Fetlar.

Contact Visit Shetland

☎ 08701 999 440

e: info@visitshetland.com

There is a small airport on Fetlar.

Places to Visit

RSPB Fetlar Nature Reserve

Baelans, Fetlar ZE2 9DJ

☎ 01957 733246

Fetlar Island is the home to 90% of the British population of red-necked phalaropes. There are also many other rare species.

Hide at Mires of Funzie

Open: Apr-Oct. No access to the actual reserve May to mid-Aug.

Fetlar Interpretive Centre *W*
Houbie
☎ 01957 733206
Open: daily, May to end-Sept;
Mon-Fri 1-5pm; Sat-Sun 2-5pm
E: info@fetlar.com

Shop, Tourist Information Centre and post office: Houbie

***W** = wet weather attraction*

Out Skerries

Little more than a few dots on most maps, the Out Skerries are home to c. 80 people living off fishing and with only a limited amount of cultivatable land on a total area of only a couple of square miles in extent. Skerry means rocky islet, a word found down the western Celtic seaboard of Britain.

A modern fish farm offers employment to a good percentage of the workers. Two good natural harbours afford shelter, all too often at a premium in the Shetlands.

Two of the three main islands – Bruray and Housay – sit snugly, conveniently allowing a bridge of 1957 to connect them together, although the road is less than a mile in length. Isolation is conveniently avoided by daily ferries and a small airstrip cuts getting there to a matter of minutes.

There is no denying that this is a tight-knit community, but it is a welcoming one, well known for its dances in its modern community hall.

The main visitors here, as on most of the Shetland islands, are migrating birds, 'twitchers' and photographers who also flock in when rare breeds drop in, having lost their sat.nav. The islands may be small, but not short on dramatic scenery and there is a B & B and self-catering accommodation available.

Getting There

Daily, from Vidlin (or Laxo in bad weather) on the Shetland Mainland, to Symbister.
☎ 01806 515226 (Voicebank 01595 743975)
There are also ferries twice a week from Lerwick.

By Air

Direct Flight operates flights from Tingwall Airport (7 miles, 11km from Lerwick), Mon, Wed & Thurs, plus Tues Apr-Sep only. On request goes via Whalsay, one flight a day, two on Thursdays.
☎ 01595 840246

Accommodation

Bookings through VisitShetland.com
☎ 08701 999440
Despite its small size, the community has plenty of visitor accommodation.

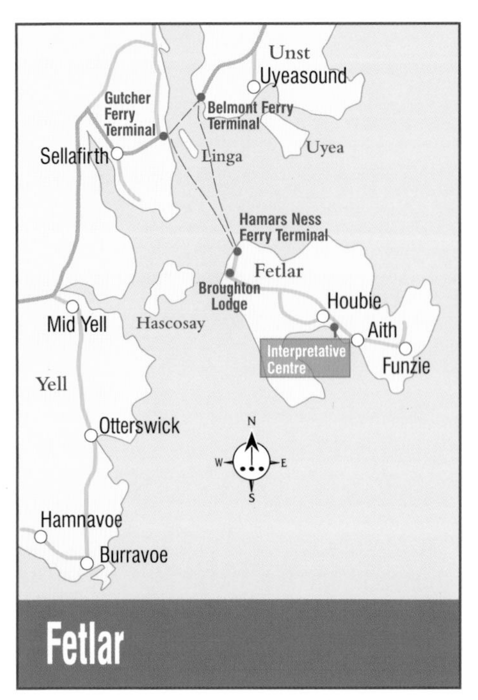

Above: Out Skerries

Above: Brough House, Fetlar

Above: North House with The Maiden Stack in the background and below: Mid-Setter and Biggins, both in Papa Stour

Papa Stour

This small island in St. Magnus Bay still provides a home for some 30 or so people. It now has an airport to overcome the roughness of the surrounding sea and even mains electricity. It is a Special Area of Marine Conservation and is noted for its sea caves, rock arches and stacks. It is a place ideal for the lovers of peace and quiet, has healthy numbers of birds and also an intriguing restoration project.

The earliest documented reference to the island is of 1299 and this refers to a specific building which existed at King Haakon's royal farm, now called The Biggins.

A partial reconstruction of the building is being undertaken with international assistance; the wooden beams etc being supplied from Granvin on the Hardangerfjord in Norway. The building will become a visitor centre upon completion.

The name Papa Stour refers to the 'island of the priests' and is a reference to an early Christian colony predating the Norsemen.

Only 2.75 miles (4.5km) in length and 2.25 miles (4km) in width, the island has several prehistoric cairns and also remains of vertical shafted watermills, where the water wheel was horizontal, near Dutch Loch.

Perhaps the most intriguing attraction is a sea cave which is actually a tunnel, accessible by a small boat from end to end, when the sea is calm. The island is best explored on foot, although the ferry carries cars.

Getting There

Shetland Islands Council ferry from West Burrafirth. The journey time is 45 minutes. Bookings ☎ 01957 722259 (Voicebank 01595 743977) Advance booking is essential.

By air

Direct Flight operates services to Papa Stour from Tingwall Airport, near Lerwick. Two flights each way, Tuesday only.

Accommodation

Holiday Cottage, East Toon
☎ 07717 517153
BackPackers Hostel, Hurdiback
☎ 01595 873229
Or Visit Shetland ☎ 08701 999 440

Unst

The most northerly populated island in the United Kingdom, Unst is further north than Bergen, Leningrad and the southern tip of Greenland. It is almost on the same latitude as Anchorage in Alaska.

VisitShetland is uncompromising in its description of Unst: "…one of the most spectacular, varied and interesting islands in Europe… Packed into an area just 12 miles long by five miles wide are stupendous cliffs, jagged sea stacks, low rocky shores, sheltered inlets, golden beaches, heathery hills, freshwater lochs, peat bogs, fertile farmland – and even a unique sub-arctic, stony desert".

The ferry is via Gutcher on Yell, just a few minutes away across Bluemill Sound to Belmont at the south-west corner of Unst. Being the island furthest north in the country leaves a lot of places labelled as the 'furthest north' in the nation, from lighthouse to public house etc.

One house worthy of note is visible as you come in on the ferry. It is Belmont House, a Georgian house attributed as being one of the finest in Scotland. Built in 1775, it had become precariously at risk until a Trust was formed to save it. The structure is now sound and Phase II of the re-furbishment has begun. Fundraising continues for the restoration of the rear porch and of course the re-furbishment, down to the last cup and curtain.

Contact: The Belmont Trust, Keldabister Banks, Bressay, Shetland ZE2 PEL

☎ 01595 820281, if you can help.

Completion is due in summer 2010.

In the south-east corner of the island is Muness, with its large, ruined castle built in 1598 by the same architect as Scalloway Castle. Admission is free and much of the building survives. The top floor was removed to provide stone for the surrounding wall! Nearby is a knitwear shop that serves tea. On the way back to the main road running north up the island is the village of Uyeasound. Down by the pier is Greenwell's Booth, a rectangular building, now roofless and built in c. 1646 as a warehouse for storing goods to sell to Hanseatic merchants from Germany who traded food and produce for local dried fish, hides, mutton etc. It is a good reminder of the sea-trade of days gone by. Situated adjacent to the pier, it was built by the 'Dutch Quay' which already was in existence. At the rear is a private youth hostel at Gardiesfauld. ☎ 01957 755279

Proceeding from Belmont on the A968 a left turn goes to Westing. Turn left here and then next left to reach Burdastuble Standing Stone, the largest in Shetland 12ft (4m) high. Lund House, built between 1725-40 is also nearby.

Scattered around Baltasound are the remains of another sea-trade, the half-century herring boom which saw employment for 10,000 people up to the 1930s. The fish were gutted and packed in barrels for export to the UK Mainland.

Baltasound is the home of the island's leisure centre, the airport and to the east, the Keen of Hamar National Nature Reserve. With the Hermaness National Nature Reserve in the north-west, Unst has two of only three National Nature Reserves in Shetland. Keen of Hamar is scheduled because of the flora growing on serpentine rock, a reserve resembling a stony desert. Hermaness is scheduled because of the seabird colony

Cottages on the shoreline, Uyeasound, Unst

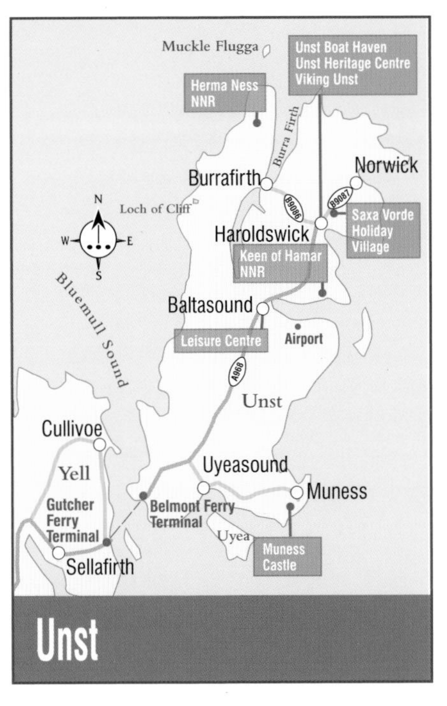

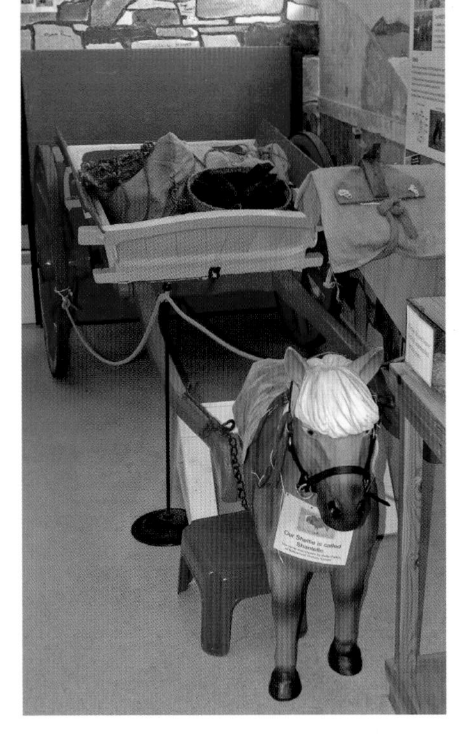

Right: Unst Heritage Centre, Haroldswick

Below: Travelling bank and village shop, Baltasound, Unst

on cliffs rising to 558ft (170m) at the Neap. Off the coast is Muckle Flugga, with its (now automated) lighthouse. Prior to automation, this was the most northerly occupied point of the United Kingdom. Just to the north of the lighthouse is the islet of Out Stack, the furthest point of all. At Keen of Hamar, look out for the Edmondston's Mouse-eared chickweed, the only site of it in the world. Hermaness has the third largest colony of great skuas and 25,000 pairs of puffins in its seabird colony of over 100,000 birds. There is parking just northwest of Burrafirth on the B9086.

Decomposed serpentine degenerates into talc, which is quarried/mined at the Clibberswick Talc Quarry near Haroldswick. It is the only working talc quarry in Britain.

There are guided walks on the two National Nature Reserves conducted by the Unst ranger.

Shetland now has its own brewery, the Valhalla Brewery, here on Unst, at Baltasound. It produces several bottled beers generally available and quite palatable too. If ever there was a local product worth supporting, a local beer ought to rank high on the list and surely this does!

North of Baltasound is Haroldswick, which in recent years has seen significant investment at the former RAF camp, creating the Saxa Vord holiday village. In Haroldswick is the Unst Boat Haven, which should not be missed. In addition to the boats, there is a large collection of all manner of things concerned with the sea and fishing. The oldest of the boats (there are currently 22) dates from c. 1868 and the latest, from 1993, a replica sixareen (six oared) boat, in use until 2002. There is a lot to take in with this collection and on your author's visit, the staff member was impressive with his knowledge. This museum is run by the Unst Heritage Centre Trust and they are to be congratulated on their achievement. Your time schedule could be in jeopardy here.

The Trust also has a nearby local heritage centre and on the entrance to the village from Baltasound is the *Skidbladner*, a recreation of a Viking ship.

Getting There

Ferry to Ulsta, Yell and then from Gutcher (Yell) to Belmont (Unst)
☎ 01957 722259
Takes 10 minutes, advanced booking advisable

By Air
Tingwall airport,
☎ 01595 840246
Sumburgh airport, Shetland

By Bus
Daily bus service
Lerwick-Unst, (not Sundays)

Accommodation

Saxa Vord
Holiday village on site of former RAF base with self-catering houses, hostel, restaurant and bar. Also VisitShetland Booking Service ☎ 08701 999440

Places to Visit

Muness Castle,
Nr, Uyeasound
Built 1598, now a ruin. Free

Hermaness National Nature Reserve & Visitor Centre
Shore Station, Burrafirth
☎ 01957 711278
e: hermaness_nnr@snh.gov.uk
Open: mid-Apr to mid-Sep; Mon-Sun 9am-7pm
Visitor Centre in former lighthouse shore station

The Keen of Hamar NNR
Baltasound
Turn off A968 just out of Baltasound on road to Haroldswick. (By decorated Bobby's bus shelter). Park at Littlehamar. Guided walks available from Scottish Natural Heritage ☎ 01959 693345 or the Ranger Service ☎ 01595 694688

Viking Unst
☎ 01595 694688
e: info@shetlandamenity.org
w: vikingshetland.com
Replica Viking boat, the *Skidbladner*, near Haroldswick, with Viking-longhouse. Also excavations at Hamar.

Farmer's Market
Baltasound Hall
Tends to be last Sun in month, Mar to Dec, confirm locally

Foord's Chocolate
Saxa Vord Resort, ZE2 9TJ
☎ 01957 711438
e: info@foordschocolates.com
Open: Tues-Sat; 1-5pm; Sun 1-4pm
Factory tour and gift shop

Muckle Flugga Charters
☎ 01806 522447
e: info@muckleflugga.co.uk
Trips to Muckle Flugga lighthouse, and Hermaness National Nature Reserve

Unst Heritage Centre ***W***
Haroldswick
☎ 01957 711528
Open: daily May-Sep; 11am-5pm
4th most visited fee charging tourist attraction in Shetland

Unst Boat Haven ***W***
Haroldswick
☎ 01957 711809
Open: daily, May-Sep; 11am-5pm
c. 20 boats are exhibited, for use with oar and sail

Unst Leisure Centre ***W***
Baltasound
☎ 01957 711577
Open: daily
Heated indoor swimming pool and good sports facilities

Other Information

Bank: weekly on a Tuesday (Bank of Scotland) at Baltasound

Cycle Hire: available at Saxa Vord General store (Skibhoul Stones)

Post Office and Fuel at Baltasound, situated together off the main road. The store also stocks local prize winning bakery products.

W = wet weather attraction

Above: Belmont House, Unst

Below: Muness Castle, Unst

Boat Haven, Haroldswick, Unst

Whalsay

Situated north-east of Lerwick, the name means whale island. You are recommended to keep a weather-eye open for them on the ferry and if you are walking along the coast. The island is 5 miles (8km) long and 2 miles (3.5km) wide. The highest point is the Wart of Clett, 393ft (120m) in height.

This isn't the most northerly isle of the nation, but it does have the most northerly golf course, at Skaw, the north-eastern part of the island. There is a healthy- sized population on the island of some 1,000 people. The main settlement is at Symbister, where the ferries arrive and this is also the heart of the island's fishing industry; there is even a white-fish processing factory here.

As on Unst, there were links with the Hanseatic League Merchants from Germany who traded with the Shetlands in the same way that they did with Norway. There is a Hanseatic Museum at the Bryggen quay in Bergen. Here on Whalsay, a warehouse survives from these times, now restored on the old quay at Symbister. The trade lasted until the Union with England in 1707, when import duties curtailed it.

At Whalsay Junior High School is Symbister House, the finest Georgian mansion in Shetland, built with granite from the Mainland. A part of the outbuildings have been converted into a museum and heritage centre.

Today the island has a new leisure and community centre, with a swimming and sports complex, near Symbister. It compliments the coastal walks, the boating club with its sailing and rowing races with a vibrant community that can trace its origins back to the Bronze Age.

Getting There

Ferry from the Mainland (Laxo) to Symbister. It takes 25 minutes and advance booking is advisable in the summer.

Symbister Terminal:
☎ 01806 566259
Booking Office: Mon-Thurs; 8.30am-1pm and 1.30-4pm (3pm on Fri). Closed Sat and Sun.

Accommodation

Booking through VisitShetland
☎ 08701 999440
Accommodation is limited, so book well in advance if you can

Places to Visit

Whalsay Heritage Centre
Symbister
☎ 01806 566422/566465
Open: end May to end of Sep, Wed, Fri-Sun 2-5pm

Golf Course: Skaw
☎ 01806 566483/566481
Most northerly golf course in UK

Leisure Centre: Symbister ***W***
☎ 01806 566678

Shopping: There are shops at Booth Park, Harldale, Sodom, Symbister

Petrol & Diesel: Available at Booth Park and Symbister

W = wet weather attraction

Yell

The second largest of the Shetland Islands, separated from the Mainland by Yell Sound. Situated 25 miles (40km) north of Lerwick, it is 17 miles (27km) long and up to 6 miles (9.5km) in width. There is a lot of moorland and it rises to 672ft (205m). The island is almost cut in two by two sea lochs, Mid Yell Voe and Whalefirth. It has a population of c. 1,000.

The Tourist Board refers to Yell as the otter capital of Britain and you may be lucky to spot these endearing creatures along the coast.This is partly due to the fact that the Yell otters are not nocturnal. In addition to seabird colonies, the moorland peat lands are home to waders, skuas and divers.

Yell is a peat-covered island with lots of moorland habitats as a result. It also has some lovely sandy beaches: West Sandwick, north of Ulsta; Breckon on the north coast; and at Gossabrough in the south-east.

Access is via the ferry from Toft on the mainland. It is only a 15 minute crossing to Ulsta.Yell is a useful base to explore Fetlar and Unst is only a ten minutes ferry crossing from Gutcher, on the north eastern coast.

There is an important broch on the east coast at Burraness. There is also a museum and exhibition centre at the Old Haa at Burravoe, a former house dating from 1672.There are not many visitor attractions on Yell, but the Old Haa should not be missed. It has a couple of memorials outside and an eclectic collection inside covering many facets of local life. It also has detail on the shipwreck *Bohus*, a German three-masted barque which ran aground nearby in 1924.There is a tea room here too.There are some fine coastal walks and much birdlife to compliment the otters.

Most of the settlements are in the east, where several harbours exist.

Getting There

Ferry from Toft on the mainland to Ulsta ☎ 01957 722259

Accommodation

Contact VisitShetland
Lerwick ☎ 08701 999440

Places to Visit

The Old Haa Museum & Exhibition Centre ***W***
Burravoe ☎ 01957 722339

Bayanne House
Sellafirth ZE2 9DG ☎ 01957 744219
Croft, workshop & prehistoric site

Burraness Broch
On the prometory south of Gutcher; one of Shetland's best

Lumbister S.S.S.I.
Established for its geology

There are several shops: at Cullivoe, Mid Yell, Aywick, Burravoe and Ulsta. Fuel is available in all of these settlements, except Burravoe, but also at West Sandwick. There is no fuel on Fetlar so check before leaving Ulsta that you have sufficient.

Leisure Centre: Mid Yell ***W***
☎ 01957 702222

Ferry at Gutcher

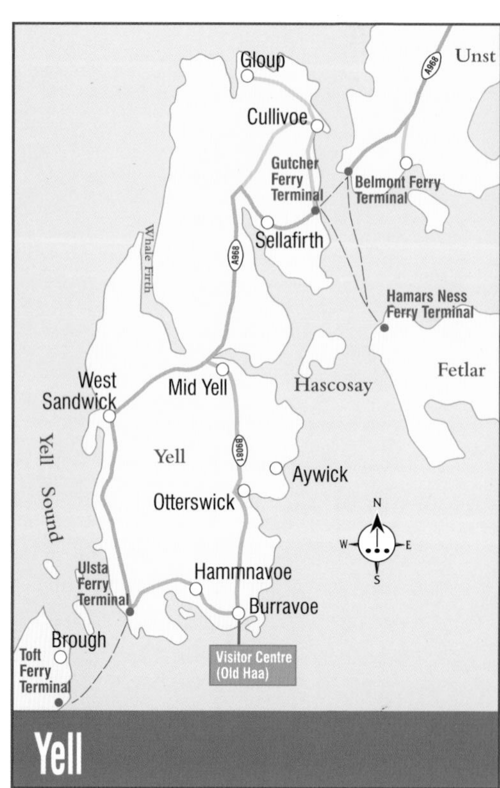

Yell

Symbister Harbour, Whalsay

Above: Muckle Flugga

Below: Fair Isle

Fair Isle

This is small island (it is 3½m/5km long and 1½m/2.4km wide) is Britain's most isolated, inhabited island. Because of its bird population, most of the island is now a conservation area with Special Protection Area status. It is situated between Shetland and Orkney and is 25miles/40km south west of Shetland at Sumburgh Head. It is owned by the National Trust for Scotland.

It is world famous for its birdlife and its Bird Observatory is 60 years old, having commenced in former huts belonging to the Admiralty. It offers accommodation for up to 30 visitors and is a mainstay of the island's economy. A new observatory, budgeted at £4m is planned, of which the island needs to raise £1½m. If you are sympathetic to the Bird Observatory Trust's work and feel able to contribute, write to them; Fair Island, Shetland ZE2 9JU, ☎ 01595 760258. The Bird Observatory is open 1st May - 31st October.

Today, some 70 people live on the island, chiefly engaged as a crofting community. The more fertile area is in the south with sheep rearing the principal activity for meal and wool. The latter is used in the manufacture of Fair Isle knitted wear. The northern part of the island is higher and covered with moorland, with high cliffs at the northern coast. Some fishing is done, for local consumption, although lobsters and crabs are treated as a cash crop and sold in Shetland.

There is an island mailboat based on the island with three ferries a week in summer (and one in winter) to Grutness near Sumburgh in Shetland (the *Good Shepherd IV*).It carries 12 passengers and the trip takes 2½ hours. The sea is notoriously rough and even when it is moderate, at least by Fair Isle standards, you may have opportunity to regret not flying in from Shetland (by Loganair). In fact in between trips the boat (*Good Shepherd IV*), is pulled from the water as the seas can be so rough. Fortnightly, the ferry is extended to Lerwick on Thursdays in the summer from May.

Getting There

Sumburgh – Fair Isle

Mid April - Mid September. Bookings cancelled because of the weather may be arranged for the next 'suitable' day. Advance booking strongly recommended. Runs on Tuesday, Thursday and Saturday.See www.shetland.gov.uk/ferries for up-to-date ferry timetables.
☎ 01595 750363 and ☎ 01595 743973 for Voicebank up-to-date ferry information.

By Air
Loganair ☎ 08457 733377

Accommodation

Fair Isle Observatory Lodge
☎ 01595 760258
e: fairisle.birdobs@zetnet.co.uk

Upper Leegh
☎ 01595 760248
w: www.extramilescotland.co.uk

Springfield (self catering)
☎ 01595 760225

South Lighthouse
Stay in the 1892 built lighthouse
☎ 01595 760355
e: info@southlightfairisle.co.uk

Auld Haa Guest House
☎ 01595 760349
e: auldhaaguesthousefairisle.co.uk

Other Information

The island has a museum, golf course, community hall and a primary school (older children go to Lerwick).

Fair Isle Activity Holidays

Shetland Wildlife Adventures
Longhill, Maywick, Shetland ZE2 9JF
☎ 01950 422483
Open 9-5pm, Mon - Fri; 11-2pm on Sat.
e: info@shetlandwildlife.co.uk

Above: South Lighthouse, Fair Isle

Above: North Lighthouse, Fair Isle

Opposite page: The cliffs at Kame, Foula are the second highest in Britain

Foula

Twenty miles west of Walls in Shetland lies one of the most isolated islands in Britain. It is 3½m/6km in length and 2½m/4½km wide and supports a population of 30. The economy is based on tourism and crofting, mainly Shetland sheep and ponies.

Approached from Shetland, the immediate hinterland is low lying, rising towards the west. There are five hills and steep cliffs to the west coast. In fact the highest one - Kame - is 1,220 ft/370m high - the second highest in Britain. Rising from the sea is the phenomenal Gaada Stack, a natural arch 130ft/39m high. There are four main crofting communities: you land at Ham, in the middle of the east coast where there is a Post Office and school. To the south is Hametun and to the north are Harrier and the Nort Toons.

The wildlife as elsewhere in the Scottish islands is dominated by the birdlife. Foula from old Norse 'Fugley' is home to the largest colony of Great Skuas in Britian and there are large populations of many other seabirds. There is a unique species of field mouse (Mus Thulensis) and the Foula sub-species of the shetland sheep. Foula means 'bird island'.

The sensitive environment has seen a succession of designations aimed at protecting the island and its wildlife. Island Special Protection Area status was followed by the award of an SSSI for the plantlife and bird colonies, followed by a National Scenic Area Award and a separate coastline SSSI for the geomorphology.

The weather dominates everything - what you do and when you arrive. There is little shelter for boats and all of them are pulled clear of the water - even the mailboat. Fortunately, there is a small airstrip which offers perhaps a more comforting means of arrival, especially when stormy seas threaten.

Islanders still hold some 'feast days' by the old Julian calendar, 12 days behind the corrected Gregorian calendar observed by the rest of the country. Examples of these are Yule – Foula Christmas – on 6th January, Newerday on 13th January and Hallowe'en on 13th November.

Recognising the value of tourism within the protective environmental designations covering the island, Scottish Natural Heritage pays for two residents to act as job-share rangers to assist visitirs and protect valuable habitats and species. They are Isobel Holbourn (☎ 01595 753233) and Sheila Gear (☎ 01595 753236).

Five months after the loss of *RMS The Titanic* her sister ship *RMS The Oceanic* was wrecked off Foula on 8th September 1914. She hit a notorious shallow reef (The Shaalds of Foula) in calm seas as a result of navigational error. Everybody was taken off and a fortnight later she slipped under the surface in a storm. In the 1970s, divers salvaged the propellors and valuable metals from the wreck site which was considered to be undiveable because of the strong tides.

Getting There

Atlantic Ferries Ltd
Aronnack, Whiteness, Shetland
ZE2 9LL
☎ 07881 823732
w: www.atlanticferries.co.uk
The vessel is based in Foula.

Sailings from Walls on Tues and Thurs plus Sat in summer to Walls and Scalloway.
Sailings info voicebank
☎ 01595 743976
Takes 12 passengers and is weather dependent. Takes 2 hours 15 minutes.

By Air
Directflight Ltd
Tingwall Airstrip
☎ 01595 840246
Flights on Mon, Tues, Wed & Fri.

Charters

Cycharters Ltd
☎ 01595 693434 (the Shetland Tourist Office, Lerwick)
Scalloway - Foula, Wed 9.30 and return 5pm
w: www.cycharters.co.uk
1½ hour journey, with trip around island and 2½ hour stay.

Accommodation

Guest House
Mrs Marion Taylor, Leraback, Foula
☎ 01595 753226

Ristie Self Catering
Mrs Isobel Holbourn
Freyers, Foula
☎ 01595 753233

Above: Airport, Foula

Below: Foula Sheep

Above: Nortend shore, Foula

Below: Gaada Stack at sunset, Foula

Fact File

Tourist Information Centre

Visit Shetland
Market Cross, Lerwick ZE1 0LU
☎ 01595 693434/08701 999440

Accommodation

Contact the Tourist Information Centre ☎ 01595 693434

Camping bods – good low cost accommodation in heritage buildings
Shetland Amenity Trust
☎ 01595 694688
e: shetamenity.trust@zetnet.co.uk
Lighthouse keeper's cottage – Eshaness, Sumburgh, Bressay
Contact Shetland Amenity Trust (see above)

Youth Hostel
King Harald St, Lerwick ZE1 0EQ
☎ 01595 692114
5* hostel

Banks

Bank of Scotland
☎ 01595 732200

Clydesdale
☎ 01595 695664

Royal Bank of Scotland
☎ 01595 694520

Lloyds TSB
☎ 01595 693605

Travelling Banks operate across the main islands

Car Hire

Bolts
☎ 01595 693636
e: info@boltscarhire.co.uk

Gairs
☎ 01595 693246
w: www.gair.co.uk

Grantfield
☎ 01595 692709
e: admin@grantfieldgarage.co.uk

Star
☎ 01595 692075
e: info@starrentacar.co.uk

Chemists

Boots
☎ 01595 692619

Laings
☎ 01595 692579/693502

Cycling

Visit Shetland produces a good and free leaflet *Cycling in Shetland Twenty Cycle Routes*

Events

Up Helly Aa Fire Event
Shetland is known worldwide for the burning of a replica Viking boat each year, last Tuesday of January.

Book Festival, September

Food Festival
Early October, for several days
w: www.shetlandfoodfestival.com

Johnsmas Foy
Shetland's summer festival held in June
w: www.johnmasfoy.com

Shetland-Bergen Yacht Race, June

Flag Day Parade, Lerwick, June

Taste of Shetland, June

Nature Festival, July

Pony Breed Show, August

Music Festivals

Accordian & Fiddle Festival, October

Blues Festival, August

Country Music, November

Folk Festival, early May

Guitar Festival, September

Islesburgh Exhibition, concerts & dance

Creative Connections
Shetland Arts, Toll Clock Centre, North Road, Lerwick
☎ 01595 743843
Music, fiddle festival, creative arts in August

Unst Festival, July
w: www.unstfest.org

Ferries

Northlink
☎ 0845 6000449
Aberdeen – Kirkwall (Orkney) – Lerwick; Scrabster (Scottish mainland) – Stromness
e: info@northlinkferries.co.uk
w: northlinkferries.co.uk

Ferry Services in Shetland
Mainland (Lerwick) – Bressay (Maryfield)
Mainland (Lerwick) – Skerries
Mainland (Vidlin) – Skerries
Mainland (Laxo) – Whalsay (Symbister)
Mainland (Vidlin) – Whalsay (Symbister)
Mainland (Toft) – Yell (Ulsta)
Mainland (W. Burrafirth) – Papa Stour
Mainland (Walls) – Foula
Mainland (Grutness, Sumburgh) – Fair Isle
Mainland (Lerwick) – Fair Isle
Whalsay (Symbister) – Skerries
Yell (Gutcher) – Unst (Belmont)
Yell (Gutcher) – Fetlar (Hamarsness)
Unst (Belmont) – Fetlar (Hamarsness)

Flights

British Airways
☎ 01950 460345 (operated by Loganair)

Direct Flight
Tingwell Airport
☎ 01595 840306
w: www.directflight.co.uk
Inter-island flights. Flights: Tingwall-Fair Isle, Out Skerries, Foula and Papa Stour. Sumburgh-Fair Isle.

Leisure Centres

Shetland has eight leisure centres, of which the largest is that serving the Lerwick area and situated on the south-west outskirts of town. All of these centres were built using revenues from oil. The largest, the Clickimin Centre at Lerwick, has a swimming pool (25m), flumes etc; sauna and spa centre etc; sports hall; bowls hall; fitness centre; café. Outside are sports pitches, athletics area and a good sized caravan (with hook-ups) and camping site. The sites are:
Aith, West Mainland
Baltasound, Unst
Brae, North Mainland
Clickimin Leisure Centre, Lerwick
Mid Yell, Yell
Sandwick, South Mainland
Scalloway Pool
Symbister, Whalsay

Public Transport

For full detail of times for ferries, air services, bus services, ask for the Directory of Shetland's Transport at Visit Shetland Tourist Information Centre.

Ranger Services

Fair Island Bird Observatory Trust
Fair Island ZE2 9JU
☎ 01595 760258

Foula Heritage
Freyers, Foula ZE2 9PN
☎ 01595 753233

Haroldswick
Unst, ZE2 9EF
☎ 01957 711528

Shetland Amenity Trust
Sandwick ZE2 9HL
☎ 01950 460403

Taxis

☎ 01595 690069/465767/422207/744214

Parking

in Lerwick town centre is chiefly on street parking in a disc zone. Discs are available from TIC or most shops.

Wildlife

For information on the natural history of Shetland, go to Nature – Shetland.co.uk. (Thanks to Helen Moncrief for her assistance).

RSPB Shetland
☎ 01950 460800

Tours

Cycharters
John Tulloch, 1 Bloomfield Place, Lerwick ZE1 0PH
☎ 01595 696598
Trips to Foula & Scalloway Isles. Evening trips to various uninhabited islands. Bookings through Visit Scotland.
4* attraction

Island Trails
Visit Scotland
Market Cross, Lerwick ZE1 0LU
☎ 01595 693434
Open: all year
Tour of old Lerwick

Shetland Geo Tours
Bookings ☎ 01595 859218 or Visit Scotland
Guided walks or scenic tours on the Mainland, Bressay, Yell, Unst, Fetlar & Whalsay

Shetland Nature
Midhouse, Northdale, Fetlar, Shetland ZE2 9DJ
☎ 01595 693434 (TIC Lerwick)
Out of hours: ☎ 07786 982773/01957 733221
e: brydon@shetlandnature.net
w: shetlandnature.net

Shetland Sea Charters
40 Russell Cres, Lerwick
Bookings ☎ 01595 692577 or Visit Scotland
Three-hour cruise around Bressay, Noss and Green Holm Island to see seabird colonies, seals etc.
Open: all year, weather permitting

The Swan Trust
Orfasay, Gulberwick
☎ 01595 697406
skipper@theswan.shetland.co.uk

Shetland Small Group Tours
1 Carlton Place, Lerwick ZE1 0ED
☎ 01595 692080
shetlandtours@btinternet.com
Shetland tours in 8-seater vehicle
Open: all year

Shetland Wildlife
Longhill, Maywick ZE2 9JF
☎ 01950 422483
info@shetlandwildlife.co.uk
Holidays and daytrips

Seabirds-and-Seals
☎ 07595 540 224 or Visit Scotland
e: info@seabirds-and-seals.com
4* attraction

Thule Charters
63 King Harald St, Lerwick ZE1 0DJ
☎ 0787 652 2292 or Visit Scotland
e: thulecharters@btinternet.com
Open: end-Mar to end-Sep
Seatours to Muckle Fugga, Noss & Bressay Sound

South Mainland
Mousa Boat Trips
M/B Solan IV
Tom Jamieson, Leebitton, Sandwick
☎ 01950 431367
info@mousaboattrips.co.uk
Open: Apr-Sep. Free admission to the broch.
Visit world's best preserved broch. Evening trips to see storm petrels returning to roost.

Useful Addresses
Scottish Natural Heritage
Stewart Building Esplanade
Lerwick ZE1 0LL
☎ 01595 693345

Above: Cormorants, Mousa

Below: Atlantic Grey Seals, Mousa

Index